Happy Birthday Josie

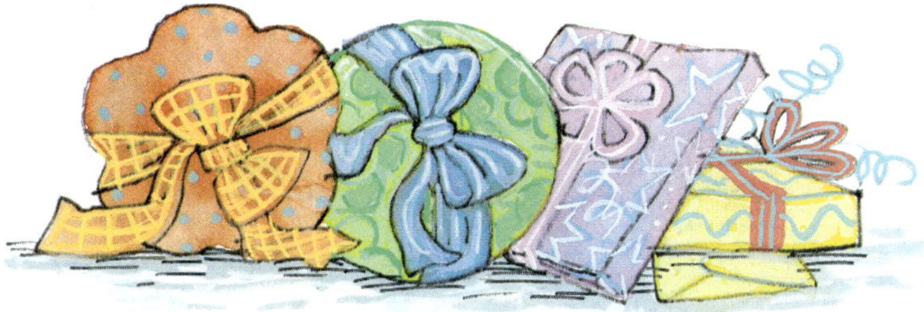

Monica Hughes
Illustrated by Lisa Smith

RIGBY

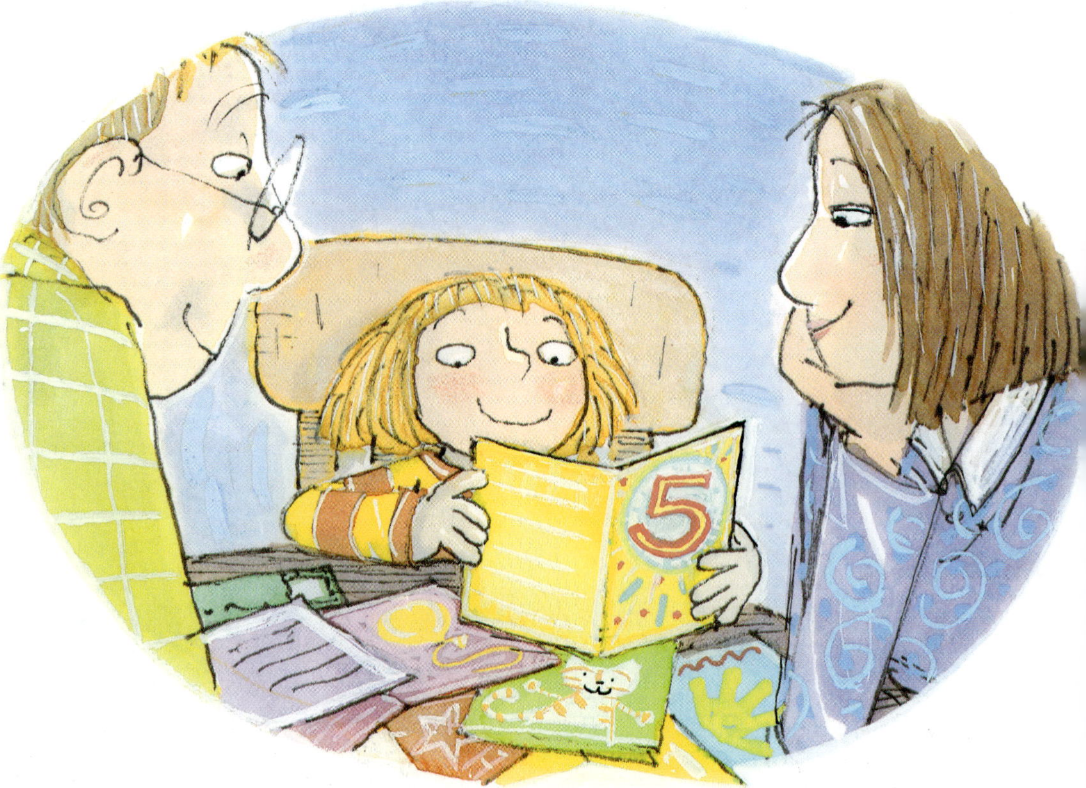

my cards

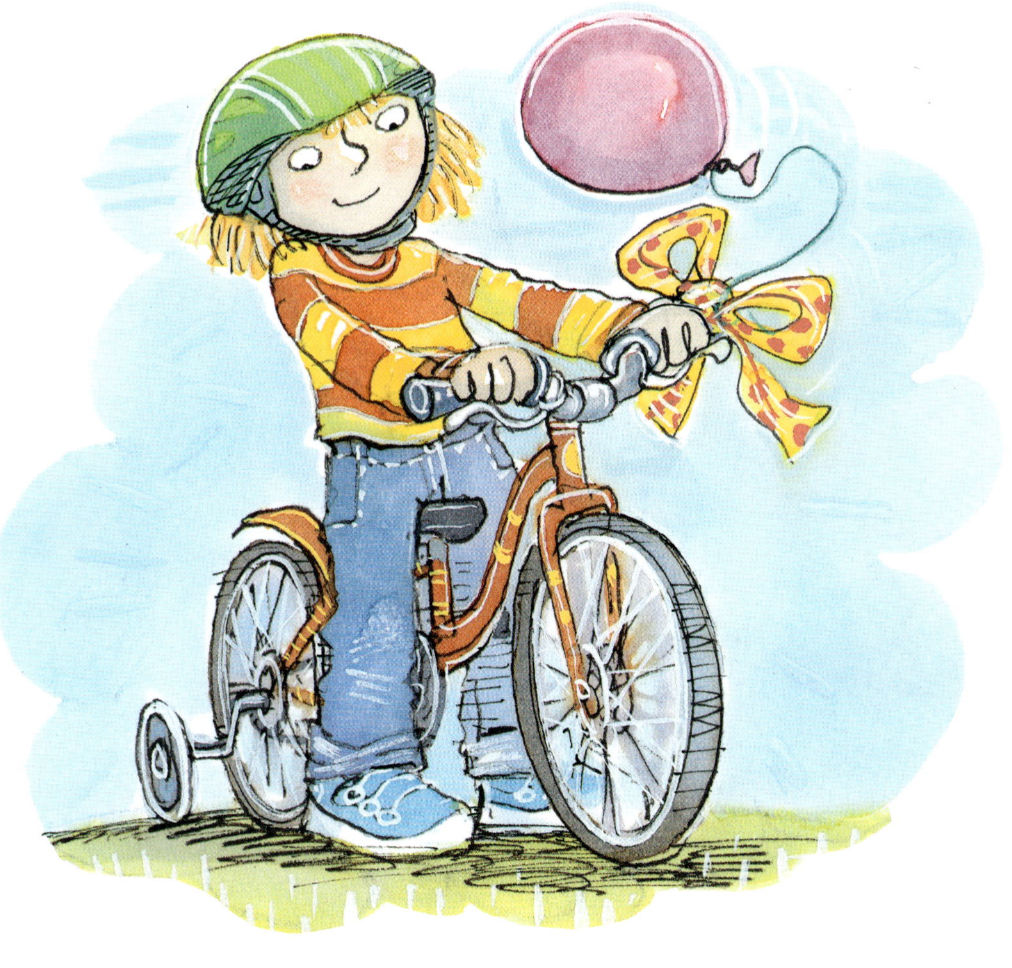

my bike

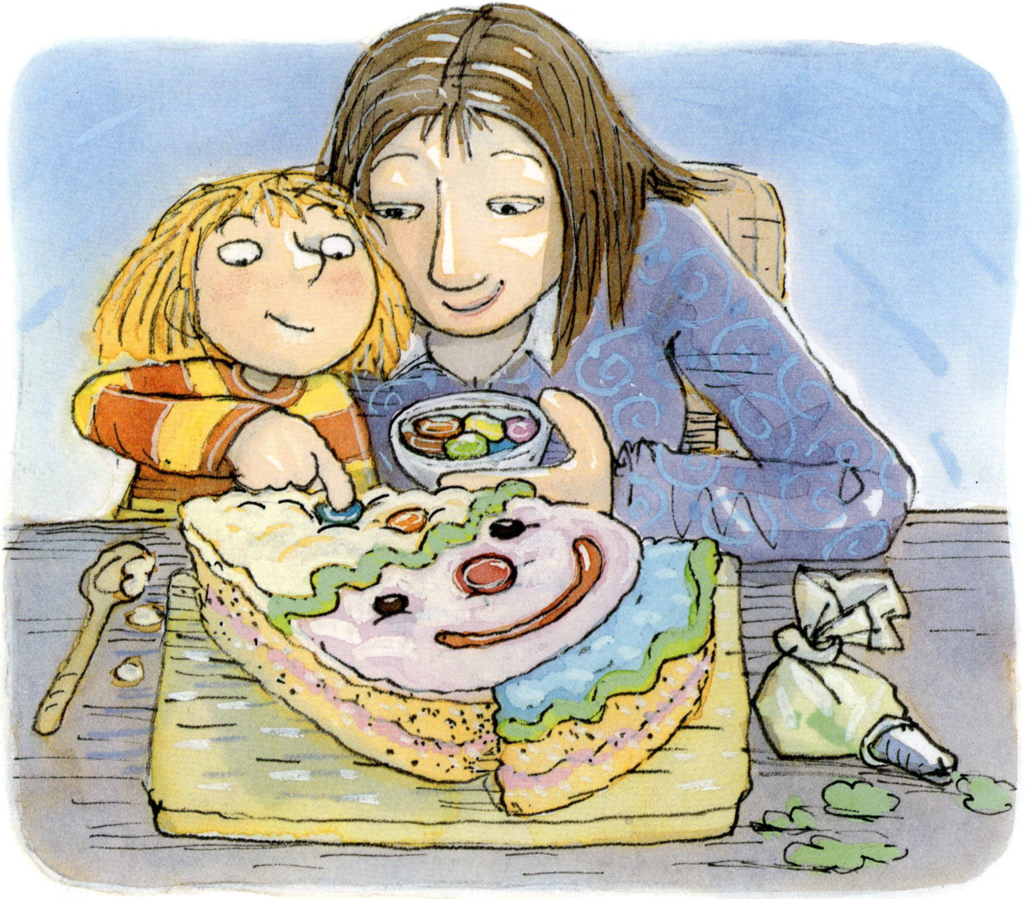

my cake

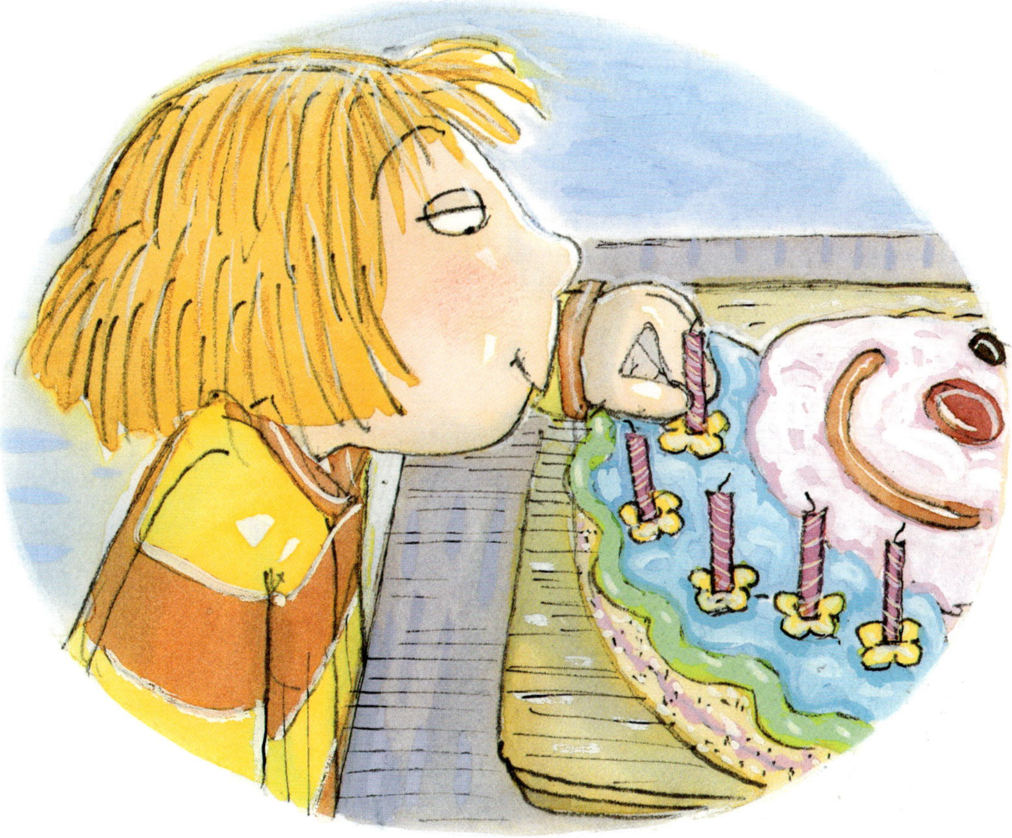

my candles

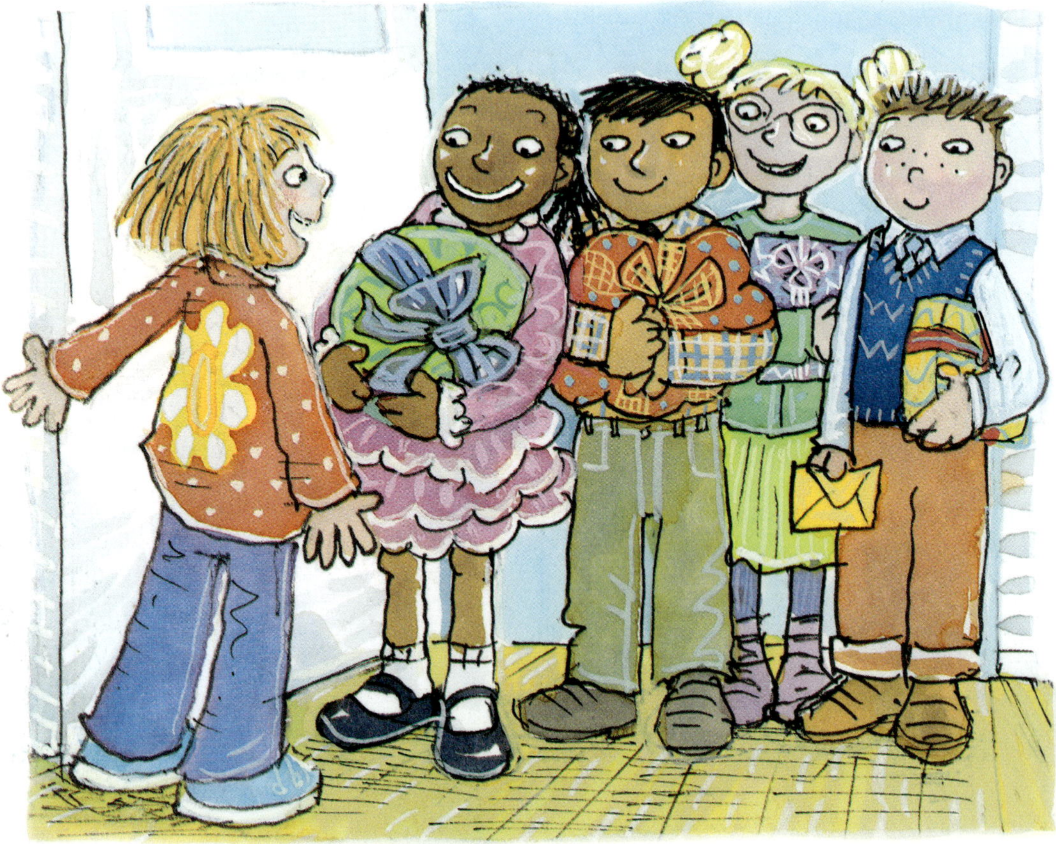

my friends

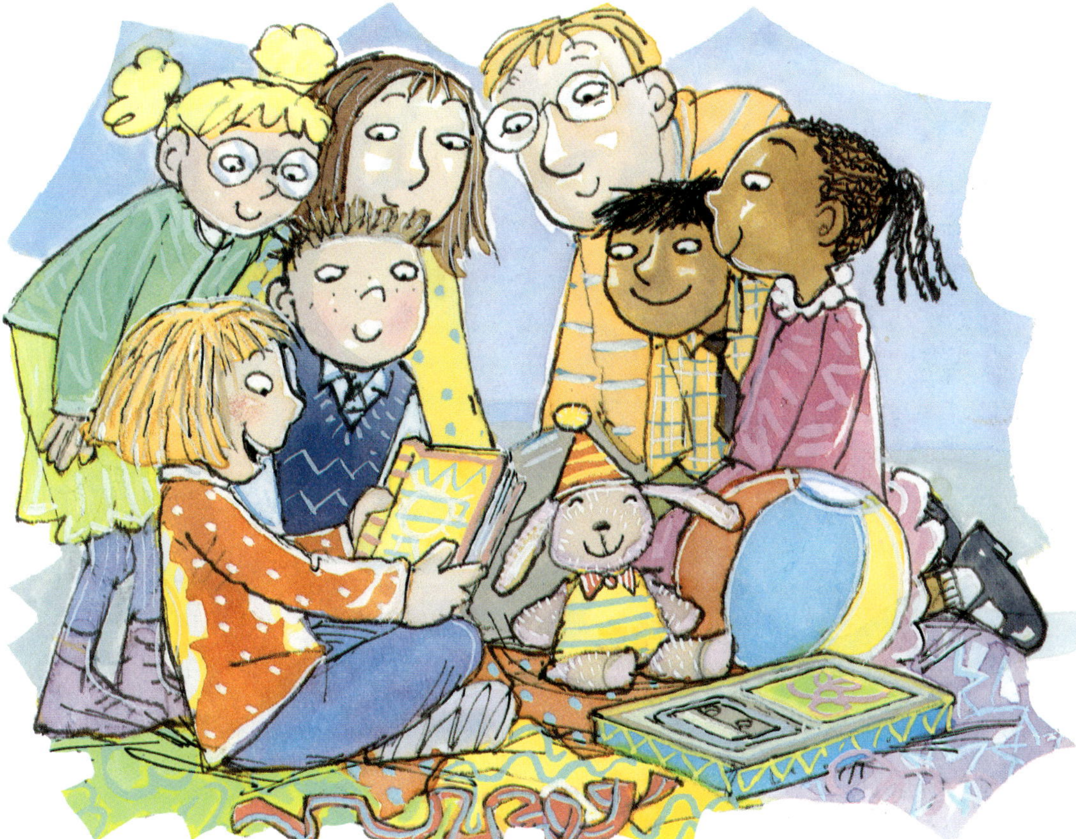

my presents

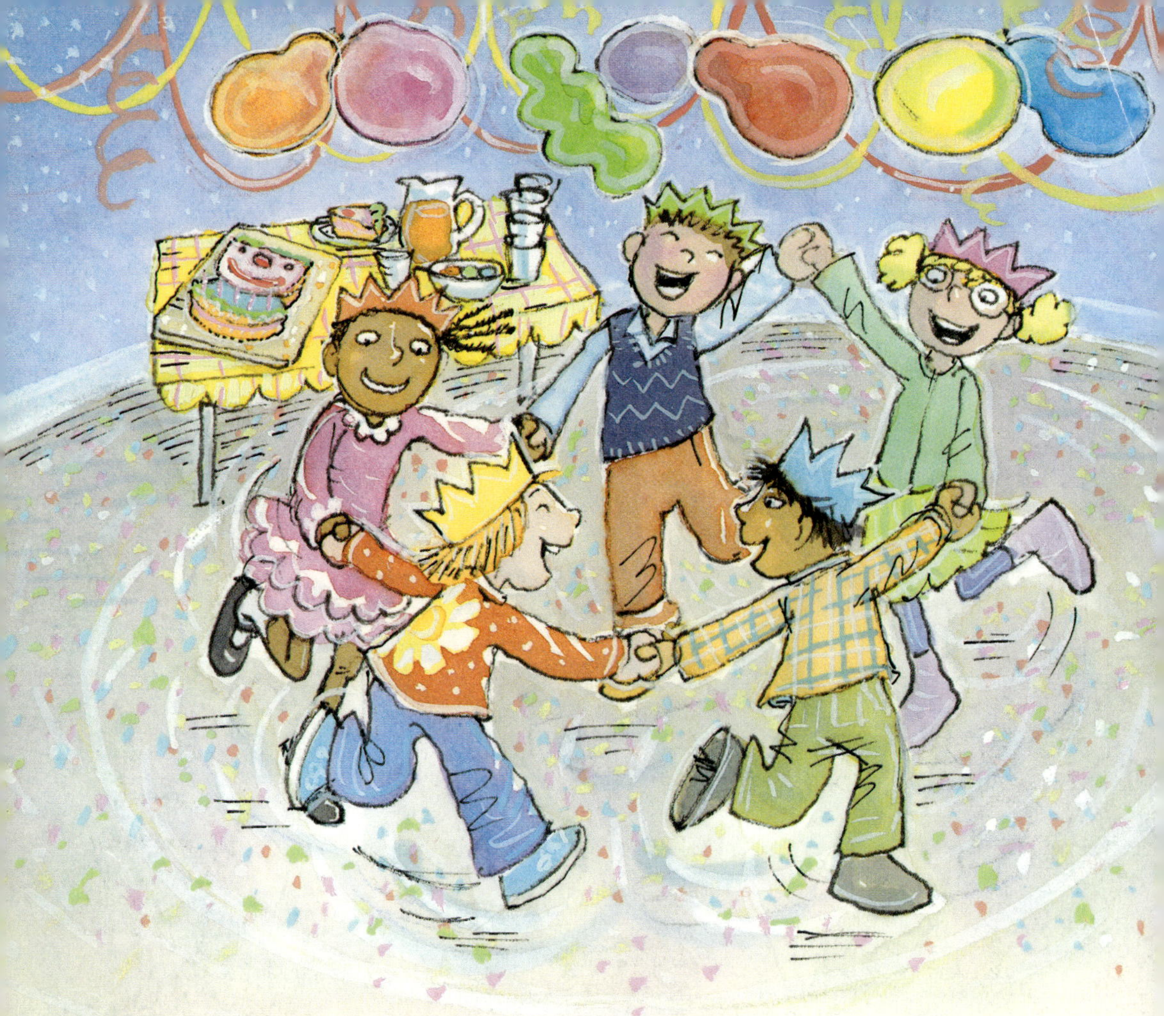

my party